ISBN 978-1-331-21015-3
PIBN 10158792

This book is a reproduction of an important historical work. Forgotten Books uses
state-of-the-art technology to digitally reconstruct the work, preserving the original format
whilst repairing imperfections present in the aged copy. In rare cases, an imperfection in
the original, such as a blemish or missing page, may be replicated in our edition. We do,
however, repair the vast majority of imperfections successfully; any imperfections that
remain are intentionally left to preserve the state of such historical works.

# 1 MONTH OF
# FREE
# READING

## at

## www.ForgottenBooks.com

By purchasing this book you are eligible for one month membership to ForgottenBooks.com, giving you unlimited access to our entire collection of over 700,000 titles via our web site and mobile apps.

To claim your free month visit:

www.forgottenbooks.com/free158792

# THE IRISH QUESTION

## *Federation or Secession*

BY

## F. S. OLIVER

Author of "ALEXANDER HAMILTON", etc.

*Reprinted from*

### The London Times

*and from*

### The London Observer

=

*With the Compliments of*
PROFESSOR W. MACNEILE DIXON
[University of Glasgow]

=

Applications for additional copies should be addressed to
### Lt. Col. G. G. WOODWARK
511 FIFTH AVENUE, NEW YORK

# ULSTER AND A FEDERAL SETTLEMENT

## I. THE OPPOSITION TO HOME RULE

This article is not to be taken throughout as an expression of the writer's own opinion, but as an attempt to understand the mind of the Ulster Protestant Party in regard to proposals for the self-government of Ireland. The object of what follows is to discover if there is any method, consistent with the principles of the Northern community, which offers a present hope of ending an old and bitter controversy.

### THE PROTESTANT COMMUNITY OF ULSTER

The population of the whole of Ireland is a little under four and a half millions, while that of the Province of Ulster is a little over one and a half millions. The Protestants of Ulster number more than 885,000 persons. They are therefore in a majority of nearly 200,000 over their Roman Catholic fellow-countrymen in the Northern Province.

The so-called "Ulster Party" is not a party in the ordinary sense of the term. It is made up of all classes of society and of every shade of political opinion. It includes Conservatives and Liberals; but Radicals, Labour men, and Socialists form by far the larger portion of it.

The Ulster Protestants have at all times been distinguished by habits of thrift, industry, and enterprise, both as tillers of the soil and in mercantile pursuits. They have been distinguished also by the importance which they attach to education and by the liberality, untainted by corruption, of their municipal administration.

At the date of the Union (1800) Belfast was a small town of less than 50,000 inhabitants; it now numbers over 400,000. The mightiest vessels launched from its slips float on every sea. Nor has this city any natural advantages, such as are derived from adjacent deposits of coal and iron, to account for its progress. While the Dublin Corporation is a byword for jobbery and incompetence, and enjoys an unenviable notoriety among the great cities of the Empire for its neglect of the very elements of health and decency among its poorer inhabitants, Belfast, with an approximately equal population presents a remarkable contrast in every particular.

For upwards of a century the Ulster Protestants have lived and worked under precisely the same conditions—economic, social, and political—as the rest of Ireland. They have prospered under the Union to no less a degree than Great Britain; and for one reason only—because of their determination to make the best of their conditions as they found them.

### THE FORCE OF SENTIMENT

Had the rest of Ireland acted on the same principles they would have prospered equally. They might even have surpassed the prosperity of Ulster by reason of their remarkable gifts of quickness and adaptability. In saying this it is not intended to cast any reproach. The force of sentiment in developing the qualities of a race and in stimulating its efforts is a factor which cannot be ignored. In the case of Ulster, love of the Union has given this force full play. Unfortunately, the sentiment which has inspired the Protestants of Ulster has not been shared by a large minority in that province and by a large majority in the kingdom of Ireland. Can we devise some re-arrangement of our institutions which will unite all Irishmen in a common bond of loyalty and good will?

## REASONS OF ULSTER'S OPPOSITION TO HOME RULE

As citizens of the United Kingdom—determined at all costs to maintain their citizenship of the Union—the Ulster Protestants have opposed Home Rule, because they believe that the present system of a single Parliament gives the best security for national safety and for just and honest government. They believe that to put an educated and progressive community under the absolute control of an overwhelming Roman Catholic majority—the greater part of whom are backward in education and industry, and are also very largely under the influence of their priesthood—would be fraught with danger, not only to the material well-being of the Protestant community, but to the education of their children and to their free institutions.

## THE PRINCIPLE OF NATIONALISM

When Ulstermen are asked to accept what is called "the *principle* of Nationalism" they usually reply that they cannot do so, because they have never yet seen any statement of this supposed "principle" which possesses real consistency, or which in any way supports the extreme claims of the "Nationalist" Party. For if it is right that the destinies of Ireland should be settled upon the formula of "self-determination," every argument which can be advanced in favour of the severance of Ireland from Great Britain can be used with equal force in favour of the severance of the six north-eastern counties of Ulster from Ireland. For these six north-eastern counties contain a large and compact majority of people who are in reality much more closely knit by ties of tradition, religion, and even of race, to the inhabitants of England and the Lowlands of Scotland than they are to the inhabitants of Munster, Leinster, and Connaught.

If, therefore, such differences in tradition, religion, and race (which, we presume, are what "Nationalism" means) are to be accepted as sufficient reason for separate political institutions, then the six north-eastern counties of Ulster would have a clear right to determine their own destinies apart from the rest of Ireland—either as a part of Great Britain, or as a distinct unit. "While, therefore," the Ulsterman would say, "we acknowledge in the most friendly spirit the ties of comradeship and local patriotism which bind us to Irishmen of the south and west, we must admit frankly—if we are driven to adopt these pernicious tests of tradition, religion, and race—that they are weaker ties than those which bind us to our fellow Englishmen and fellow Scotsmen. And they are infinitely weaker than those ties which bind us to the United Kingdom as a whole. Our citizenship of that Union is the thing of all others which we are most proud of, most attached to, most determined to preserve at whatever cost."

## EFFECTS OF THE WAR

It is not easy for anyone who has not lived in Ireland during the war to realize the effect which has been produced upon the minds of the Protestants of Ulster by the words and deeds of those in whose hands it is now

4

proposed to place their destinies. The greater part of the people of Ireland have failed to do their part in the war. In many instances they have insulted and injured those who *have* done their part in it. They have engaged in a rebellion. They continue to agitate and to hold meetings, even in Belfast, at which they openly rejoice over what they describe as the defeats of the Allies. Is it strange that these occurrances inspire their Protestant fellow-countrymen with increased horror at the thought of being put under their rule?

The rebellion took place at a time which made it not merely treachery to the State, but to the cause of freedom. It was marked by the worst atrocities. Unarmed and unsuspecting persons were shot down and stabbed to death by the rebels as ruthlessly as Belgian peasants by the German soldiery. It is true that those concerned in this rebellion were a small minority; but it is equally true that, shortly after the event, they were acclaimed as heroes by a large, if not by the larger, part of the Irish people.

This fickleness and instability of opinion, this tendency to swing round and change allegiance in a sudden excitement, are what their fellow-countrymen in the North dread, perhaps more than anything else in the proposal to subject Ulster to an Irish Parliament. The Protestant community is not blind to the qualities of the South and West—their quick intelligence, their generous impulses, their courage in battle; but the uncertainty of their attachments and their changing moods fill Ulster with misgiving, and make it necessary to insist upon the fullest securities.

The official Nationalists did indeed condemn the rebellion; but the rebels now claim to be the leaders of a dominating majority, and the results of recent elections appear to justify their pretensions.

The professions of fair treatment with which the official Nationalists have endeavoured to allay opposition to Home Rule have failed to impress Ulster. Their words are constantly being contradicted by their actions; as, for instance, a few mnths ago, during the debates on the Reform Bill, when they were found strenuously opposing a proposal for the redistribution of seats in Ireland (upon a basis of population) in order to rectify the present inequality under which the Nationalists are over-represented, and the Ulster Protestants are under-represented, in the Imperial Parliament.

Ulstermen have asked, and continue to ask, that compulsory military service should be applied to Ireland as to England and Scotland, but their opponents obstinately refuse, and threaten rebellion if such a step is taken. The result is that, whereas Scotland, with a slightly larger population, has sent 620,000 men to the Colours, only 170,000 have been sent from Ireland. This contrast is keenly felt.

Every one who has lived in Ireland knows instances in which returned soldiers—even the wounded—have been boycotted, insulted, beaten, and stoned, for no other reason than that they had dared to follow the dictates of their conscience. Faced with these manifestations of the spirit of hatred and oppression, the Ulster Protestants say frankly that they are compelled to think of their own safety and that of their families; that they cannot afford to let the whole of their available manhood enlist, lest they place themselves at the mercy of people who openly profess to regard the methods employed in the recent rebellion as models worthy of imitation.

### The Religious Question

It is impossible to deal sincerely with the Irish problem unless we are prepared to face the religious issue. Rightly or wrongly, the Ulster Protestants

5

are convinced that the policy of the Roman Church is hostile to civil and religious liberty. For holding this opinion they are frequently accused of intolerance even by their fellow-Protestants throughout the British Empire. Their reply is—(1) that they have lived side by side with a Roman Catholic majority, whereas their critics have not; (2) that they distinguish two principles in Roman Catholicism, one of which is apt to be entirely overlooked in Protestant countries.

They distinguish between the religious faith of individual Roman Catholics and the political aims of the Vatican. The former they do not impugn. They recognize fully that their Roman Catholic fellow-subjects cherish their spiritual beliefs with a sincerity no whit inferior to their own. They respect the devotion of their clergy. They would never deny that the Roman Catholics are entitled, no less than themselves, to complete freedom of worship; but for generations past Roman Catholics have in fact enjoyed not only complete freedom of worship, but complete equality in the eyes of the law.

With regard to those Roman Catholics who have joined the Army the Protestant community does not stint its praise. In becoming soldiers these have often had to endure sour looks, hard words, and cruel injuries from their own people.

None the less, Ulster maintains that it is necessary to distinguish between the piety of individual Roman Catholics—both priests and laity—and the politics of the Church of Rome. Their experience warns them that the statecraft of the Vatican is a persistent encroacher, an industrious fomenter of discord. During the past 10 years, they maintain, there has been no relaxation, but on the contrary a marked recrudescence, of its activities in the North of Ireland. And they conclude with this question:—"When we consider what has happened throughout the world during the present war, shall we discover any reasons for laying aside the opinion which is charged against us as intolerance?"

## The Sinn Fein

Another thing which confirms them in their determination not to forego their citizenship of the United Kingdom is the rapid spread of the Sinn Fein —a society which claims at the present time, probably with justice, to control a majority of the whole inhabitants of Ireland. The meaning of the name is enough in their eyes to condemn it—"For Ourselves Alone."

The Protestants of Ulster love Ireland, as a Virginian or a New Englander loves Virginia, or New England; but their loyalty to the Union comes before their attachment even to Ireland. The Sinn Fein make no concealment of their intention to reduce the connection between Ireland and Great Britain to a purely nominal tie, to a titular suzerainty—a phrase of derision and contempt—and to destroy the Union. They aim openly at Seccession. "In this conspiracy," says the Protestant community, "we will never become their accomplices, and while we have strength to resist it we will never consent to be their victims."

(Note.—A Roman Catholic critic has protested against the references in the foregoing article to "the policy of the Church of Rome" or "the Vatican"; and he maintains that "the policy of Maynooth" would be a more correct description. I wish to point out, however, that I do not profess to have set out my own views of this matter, but only to have tried to give an accurate account of the opinions of the Ulster Protestants.)

## II. "DOMINION STATUS"

In the preceding article the general nature of the opposition of the Protestants of Ulster to Home Rule has been considered, and also the particular effect which recent experiences—the rebellion, the opposition to military service, the treatment of returned soldiers, the supposed policy of the Vatican, and the attitude of Sinn Fein—have had in strengthening their original opposition.

### Dominion Status

It is clear that the form of self-government which is most favoured by the Nationalist Party and Sinn Fein is "Dominion Status."

Upon these principles Ireland would be given the same degree of independence that is possessed by Canada, Australia, New Zealand, and South Africa. She would not be one of the federated States of the United Kingdom —as Quebec is one of the federated States of Canada, or as New South Wales is one of the federated States of Australia, or as Virginia and Massachusetts are federated States of the U. S. A.—but she would become virtually separate, free at any moment to shake off the British connection and to go her own way in peace or war.

This proposal may be compared to a demand on the part of the South Island of New Zealand to separate from the North Island; or to that other demand, made by certain Southern States of the American Union, to break away from their Northern neighbours, which was refused and defeated half a century ago.

The Protestants of Ulster would admit that "Dominion Status" is a right and reasonable arrangement in the case of territories which are situated thousands of miles away from the Mother Country, and whose declaration of their absolute independence, though it might wound our feeling and diminish our strength, would not necessarily be fatal to our very existence. But who, they ask, that regards the safety of the United Kingdom, or of Great Britain, can contemplate placing Ireland in such a position except as an act of national suicide? Suppose Ireland to have been under an Independent Government, and suppose that Government to have been hostile or neutral in the present war, what chance would British shipping have had against swarms of enemy submarines sheltering in her territorial waters? This proposition, they say, needs only to be stated in order to be instantly rejected by any mind which is capable of grasping the realities of the situation.*

### Representation of Protestants

Another matter which has been canvassed in the Press is the proposal for safeguarding the position of Protestants by giving them representation in the Irish Parliament either greatly in excess of their just proportion or by means of

---

* Herr Bacmeister, the Prussian Deputy, in *Das Grössere Deutschland*, the chief Pan-German periodical (May 31st) :— . . . . "What seems more important to us is that recognition of the community of interests between Germany and Ireland, as against England, should be brought much more to the front among us than has hitherto been the case. A free Ireland is a bulwark of the freedom of the seas—a bulwark of vital necessity for Germany. We do not know whether the British statesmen are right in asserting a connection between Irish revolutionary feeling and German propaganda. But in such a connection we should see no sign of a bad German policy."

nominated members. In the opinion of Ulster both of these suggestions are futile. What security could there be in any fancy arrangement of either kind? What chance could either of them have of permanency, seeing that both are founded on injustice? There is no section of society in the British Isles more attached to the democratic principle than the Protestants of Ulster. With what self-respect could they consent to shelter behind this ridiculous make-believe? They do not ask for over-representation, but only that they may enjoy the security afforded by the unfettered supremacy of the United Kingdom Parliament. Nominated members having no popular support behind them would carry no weight. And, looking to the future, who would nominate? The Crown or some party caucus? This proposal also, they say, only needs to be looked in the face to be rejected.

## Administrative Safeguards

Unjust administration is regarded by Ulstermen as being at least as great a danger as oppressive legislation. In particular, they fear "jobbery" to public posts; political appointments of Judges and magistrates unqualified or unwilling to give just decisions; party appointments of police officers who will not enforce the law for the protection of the minority; mis-spending of public money on works which are designed, not for the general benefit of the community, but for the enrichment of contractors and localities which are able to bring special influence to bear upon the Government; taxation of the thrift and industry of Ulster for the support of classes and districts which, as yet, have not learned to practise either the one virtue or the other. But beyond everything else they seem to fear the division of those resources which must be devoted to the education of their children, if the prosperity and freedom of the Ulster Protestants are to continue. And in regard to education there is an additional danger of great gravity arising out of the supposed hostility of the Roman Church to the spread of knowledge.

## General Desire for Settlement

Nevertheless, there is no section of the Irish people which professes to desire a final settlement more than the Protestant community does. Such a settlement can only be based on compromise. It is obvious that the extremists will not welcome such a settlement, for they will be content with nothing short of absolute "secession." Nor will such a settlement be welcomed by those persons whose policy it is, not to allay, but to keep alive, the grievances of Roman Catholic Ireland against Protestant Great Britain.

On material grounds alone, Ulstermen desire a settlement. They will tell you that for seven years past their progress has been hampered, because in all their plans for future development they have been haunted by the spectre of insecurity, and by the alternatives of emigration or armed resistance.

## Possibility of a Settlement

Is there any possible basis of settlement? This question has been answered more or less in the following terms by various Ulstermen with whom the writer has talked:—

"The idea of any profound change in our present Constitution is abhorrent to us. We regard the existing Union with love and veneration. A single Parliament seems to us sufficient for all purposes of good government provided that its members will loyally endeavour to make it work, and will not pervert its forms to factious uses.

"If, however, the majority of our fellowcitizens throughout the United Kingdom are of a different opinion; if they hold that, in the great and increasing complexity of our national life, one Parliament cannot hope to deal efficiently both with the domestic concerns of England, Scotland, and Ireland individually, and at the same time with those interests which are common to the whole Union; if, holding these views, they conclude that there must be delegation to a group of Subordinate Legislatures of certain powers and functions at present possessed by the United Kingdom Parliament, in order to escape from a dangerous congestion of legislation and administration; if, being of these opinions, they ask us to follow their lead, and to join with them in adopting this new system, then certainly we should find it difficult to justify a refusal, even although we differ in opinion as to the need for the proposed change.

"*But this is precisely what we have never yet been asked to do.* It has never yet been proposed to us that Ireland should join in a scheme which England, Wales, and Scotland were willing to apply to themselves. On the contrary, under all the various Home Rule Bills it has been laid down that, whereas the domestic concerns of Ireland are to be turned out and excluded from the purview of the United Kingdom Parliament, the much greater and more multifarious domestic concerns of England, Wales, and Scotland are still to remain as a burden upon its shoulders.

"Is it wonderful, in these circumstances, that the Ulster Protestants are somewhat sceptical as to the sincerity of the argument founded on congestion? If the representatives of England and Scotland were in earnest, surely they would be willing to do unto themselves what they have proposed should be done unto us. In spite, however, of their talk about the evils of congestion, they have so far never made any proposal to relieve congestion by removing their own domestic concerns from the overloaded Parliament of the Union. May we not, therefore, be forgiven for harbouring a suspicion that they are actuated, not so much by a desire for the better government of the United Kingdom as a whole, as by mere impatience to be rid, at any cost, of the vexation of listening any longer to tales of Irish discontent?"

## III.  THE PRINCIPLE EXPLAINED

In the first article the causes, both general and particular, of the opposition of the Protestants of Ulster to Home Rule were considered. In the second their reasons have been stated for rejecting "Dominion Status," even when coupled with fancy proposals for the over-representation of Unionists— a thing which they regard as opposed to the democratic principle. It has been pointed out that, although Ulstermen profess, with all sincerity, to desire a final settlement, they regard unjust administration as no less dangerous than unjust legislation. An attempt has been made to show why they have hitherto regarded as insincere the argument frequently advanced by British Liberals, in favour of Home Rule, namely, that it would relieve congestion in the Imperial Parliament.

Can the essential substance of Union be safeguarded effectively, according to Ulster ideas, under the Federal system? In this article an attempt will be made to answer that question.

## No Need for Delay

But, it is said, a true Federation cannot be made in a few weeks, and the urgency of the Irish problem brooks no delay. The same thing has been said for 30 years.

## Principles of a True Federation

The fundamental principle of a Federation is that the states or nations which compose it shall all stand in the same relation to the Central Parliament. But beyond this it is also essential that the functions which are entrusted to the subordinate Legislatures shall not be (1) such as to reduce the supremacy of the Central Parliament to a shadow, or (2) such as to put into the hands of the states or nations power to interfere in any way with the freedom of trade, transport, or travel within the limits of the Federation.

(1) Under the first of these heads it is of paramount importance that the Central Parliament of the Union should retain all powers and functions which are not expressly delegated and made over to the National Parliaments.

(2) Under the second head it is essential that Customs and Excise should be in the hands of the Imperial Parliament, for the reason that Customs and Excise are not merely the symbols of union, but are of the very essence of union. If each State has it in its power to erect tariff barriers against its neighbours, there can be no free flow of commodities between the various members of the Federation; their union will be weakened thereby, and friction, grievances, and reprisals will be certain to result.

Upon the principles of a true Federation, the United Kingdom Parliament would simultaneously delegate and make over powers and functions with regard to the domestic concerns of Ireland to an Irish Legislature, and with regard to the domestic concerns of England, Wales, and Scotland to English, Welsh, and Scottish Legislatures.

One thing, however, is certain—the Parliament of the Union must stand in the same relation to all the kingdoms of the Union. It must not be the Union Parliament as regards England, Wales, Scotland, and Ireland, and at the same time, and in addition, the National Legislature of England, Wales, and Scotland. The domestic affairs of England, Wales and Scotland must come right out and must be given into the charge of some other body or bodies. It would not be a true Federation, and it would be an entirely unworkable arrangement— open to every form of confusion and intrigue—if the Parliament of the Union stood in a different relation to Ireland on the one hand, and to England, Wales, and Scotland on the other. Every Home Rule Bill which has yet been introduced has made shipwreck upon this reef. Irish representation at Westminster has always been the fatal *crux*. So long as the principles of a true Federation are shirked as regards England, Wales, and Scotland, it will continue to be fatal. If, on the other hand, these principles are boldly applied, most of the difficulties of Irish representation will vanish.

Another thing which is essential to a true Federation is that the Parliament of the Union must possess a real supremacy, and not merely a "titular suzerainty." As love of the Union is a nobler sentiment than Irish patriotism, so, even the Ulsterman would freely admit, is love of Ireland a nobler sentiment than attachment to any particular province of Ireland. But in the probationary period, and until the fair working of self-government has been proved by experience, they would probably judge it necessary that Ulster should have, within its own sphere, a power of veto upon laws, and of control over their enforcement, in such matters as affect her vital interests.

10

To accept even a true Federation would entail a bitter sacrifice for the Ulsterman. And certainly it is quite clear that he will never accept "Secession," or any arrangement, however ingeniously disguised it may be, which heads straight for "Secession," or, by a more devious course, towards the inevitable war which he feels assured must in that case be waged sooner or later to prevent "Secession."

But is there, in fact, any reason why a true Federation, if it be desirable, cannot be made, at any rate, in a few months—in less time than the Irish Convention has already spent over its deliberations? The ground to be explored, if wider, is not more difficult—is, indeed, much less difficult—than the ground which the Irish Convention has been engaged in surveying. In the case of England and Scotland (though Wales stands on a somewhat different footing) domestic legislation and administration are, in fact, to a large extent separated at the present time. The Reform Act, which resulted from the Speaker's Conference, is proof that the very greatest constitutional changes can be effected now, while the spirit of party is in abeyance, with a speed and good will which would have been inconceivable in pre-war days.

There is an alternative; but it would be a calamity to have to fall back on it. If an Irish Parliament is so urgent that it cannot be withheld until the general federal system is made secure, this fact need not prevent agreement now upon the general form of federation which is suitable for the United Kingdom as a whole. If this were done Ulster could not object to the setting up of an Irish Legislature forthwith, providing she herself were left out until, in due course, the system was adopted by the whole of the United Kingdom. It would be an illogical arrangement, but not more illogical than any Home Rule Bill that has yet been introduced. And the exclusion of Ulster would give security that the lop-sided arrangement would be only a temporary disfigurement of our Constitution.

This alternative is bad because it delays the final settlement which is so much desired. If there must be a change, even Ulster would probably infinitely prefer that it were carried through forthwith. And is there any reason why it should not be carried through forthwith, if the statesmen of England and Scotland are in earnest about the evils of congestion and the need for improving the machinery of the Constitution?

In these articles I have endeavored to set out the views of the Ulster Protestant community as I have gathered them in various conversations. As my sources of information are necessarily limited, it is not unlikely that I may have gone astray at certain points, but in the main I believe that the statement I have given is a true one.

I wish, however, to make two things clear. In the first place, there is no pretence that the conclusion—the suggestion of a federal settlement—represents the Ulster view; it is entirely my own. In the second place, the objections of the Protestant community to any change in our present Constitution differ very widely from my own.

I do not regard federalism as the lesser of two evils. On the contrary I look upon it as a great good. I cannot see in what other way our domocratic institutions can hope to maintain themselves. Congestion of business in our Central Parliament must inevitably baffle all our efforts at reconstruction after the war, unless during the war, the beneficent forces of local effort and patriotism can be set free to work out their own salvation, according to the traditions and temper of the various communities which make up the United Kingdom. Decentralization on a great scale appears to me to be the only road to

11

safety; and federalism, so far as I can see, is the only safe method of decentralization. "Mirabeau," wrote Lord Acton, "was not only a friend of freedom, which is a term to be defined, but a friend of federalism, which both Montesquieu and Rousseau regarded as a condition of freedom. When he spoke confidentially, he said that there was no other way in which a great country like France could be free." I humbly subscribe to this opinion, and pray that, before it is too late, the method may be applied to our own case.

# FEDERAL DECENTRALIZATION

An important objection against Federalism which has presented itself to a number of acute minds is, that this principle is only applicable for bringing States or Nations into closer relations with one another than those which previously existed between them; but that it is *not* a method for devolving powers of legislation and administration from a Central Parliament to subordinate legislatures.

To a certain extent, this objection seems to be a matter of words rather than of substance.

I have no right to speak as a historian, but it seems to me that, for more than a century past, people of authority have talked and written about "federalism" (meaning what our modern Federalists mean by it), and have applied, or endeavoured to apply, what they have described as the "federal principle" in circumstances not at all dissimilar from our own. The term has been so used widely by Sir Wilfrid Laurier (1909), and it was also so used by Mr. Chamberlain when advocating his own alternative proposals during the Home Rule controversies (1885-1887); while the idea, as applicable to the United Kingdom, was recommended by Mr. Childers ten years earlier.

In Lord Acton's somewhat disjointed, but very illuminating lectures on the French Revolution, he constantly refers, and evidently with approval, to the efforts to establish a new regime in France upon the principle of Federalism, which were made by Mirabeau and others who founded their arguments upon Montesquieu, and upon the precedent of the U. S. A. Constitution which had been created a few years earlier. These people aimed at setting up provincial assemblies to deal with local matters according to the traditions and temperaments of the various distinctive regions of France, all of which had gradually become absorbed in a centralized government during the preceding three centuries. The process aimed at was constantly referred to as "federalism" at the time, and is so referred to by Lord Acton himself, who adopts the term without comment or criticism. His lectures were delivered long before 1911, when "federalism" came more or less prominently into our political discussions.

Of course, the French Federalists failed, and the consequences of their failure are notorious. Napoleon, like any other tyrant whose aim is absolute rule, pursued the policy of centralizing power, with no less rigour, though with much more vigour, than his Bourbon predecessors. Nor is it impossible, or even improbable, that the tyranny of a democracy, if once securely established upon party machinery, might act in the same way.

From the practical point of view, on the other hand, I have never been able to see any real difficulty in devolving powers from the Central Parliament upon local, provincial, or national legislatures, providing the supremacy of the Central Parliament is fully maintained (as I think it only can be fully maintained) upon the federal principle, *i.e.,* upon the principle that the Federal Power stands in precisely the same relations to each one of the federal units.

Indeed, from the practical point of view, it would seem to be much easier for a strong Central Parliament to devolve local powers, and at the same time to maintain its federal supremacy, than it ever can be to persuade independent, or semi-independent, States to come together and agree to part with enough of their respective sovereignties, in order to clothe the Federal Power with sufficient authority.

To illustrate my meaning let me put it in this way:—

(1) In a certain district we will suppose that there are a number of small farms and holdings, held on various tenures and belonging to all sorts of odds and ends of people. These units are, for the most part, exceedingly uneconomical. There is no cooperation between them, either in buying or in selling. Some people are discouraged; other people are half asleep; others again have too little capital or too few brains; and all of them are inclined to be quarrelsome, and to compete against one another, instead of combining or cooperating to make the best profit they can as a community out of the land which they attempt to cultivate. This *first* state of things we may describe as *Independent Status*.

(2) Somebody with money in his pocket comes along, likes the district, realizes the conditions and possibilities, acquires the whole property bit by bit, turns out those tenants whose methods are hopelessly unsatisfactory, carries out improvements, reclamations, and repairs on a liberal scale, and proceeds to manage the whole thing as one huge farm. The new system is a great improvement in many ways upon the old one; more and better crops are taken off the ground; more and better stock is raised. This *second* state of things we may describe as *Centralized Government.* . . . .

(3) But after a time the intelligent new proprietor begins to understand that, although for certain purposes (*e.g.,* for big, general improvements, for the wholesale buying of fertilizers, feeding stuffs, etc.; for the selling of produce), his scheme works very well, there is, nevertheless, one great flaw in it, viz., that the unit is much too big for economic farming, on this ground among others—that the initiative of the ordinary or average farmer is paralysed by the too inflexible and mechanical nature of the system. On these grounds the proprietor or land-owner-farmer comes to the conclusion that, for the purpose cf getting the best possible results, he must redivide his property into smaller economic units; for he is obliged to take average human nature and capacities into his account. Accordingly he subdivides his one huge farm; and having learned by experience, he draws his leases upon a liberal and far-sighted plan. Probably he will enter into partnership arrangements with his various farm-managers; he will retain in his own hands the power to regulate the upkeep and development of the estate as a whole; he will adhere to the system of buying fertilizers, feeding stuffs, implements, materials, etc., etc., through his own central organization, so as to get them on the very cheapest terms; he will maintain also the system of joint or cooperative disposal of produce so as to secure the highest possible prices by selling at the top of the market, etc., etc. This *third* state of things we may describe as *Federalism*.

I need not elaborate this somewhat clumsy metaphor any further. Most people who have had to deal with land will probably agree that in the circumstances which I have assumed the final policy of the land-owner-farmer could not justly be condemned as retrograde or reactionary. On the contrary, it will probably be considered quite as much an improvement on the second stage as the second stage was an improvement on the first.

This is more or less how I conceive that the federal principle would

14

work in the United Kingdom. We have to deal with average human nature —with the peculiar traditions and temperaments of different localities, just as the land-owner-farmer has to deal with the different prejudices, aptitudes, and characters of his various farm-managers.

Leaving metaphors aside and getting back to the facts, I should like also to lay stress upon the great urgency of Federal Decentralization, not so much on account of the special difficulties which are facing us in Ireland, but even more, owing to the rapidly approaching dangers of congestion in the whole United Kingdom. I need not dwell upon the magnitude and complexity of the problems which will have to be tackled immediately upon the signing of peace. Many of these, indeed, will need to be tackled during the war, as we are realizing more and more every day.

Among the latter, which are of great variety, I should certainly include such changes as may be necessary in our constitutional machinery. For these are much more easily carried through now than they will be when the war has ceased to focus public interest and subdue party spirit.

The majority, however, of these problems, which are likely to lead to congestion—if no proper means of dealing with them have been provided in the meanwhile—relate to matters of local character, which ought to be dealt with in accordance with the traditions and habits and points of view of the different parts of the United Kingdom. Under a system of Federal Decentralization the subordinate State Legislatures would be charged with these local functions.

There is another reason of an altogether different character which weighs with me, but which I will only touch upon here, because it would need many words to set it out completely. I think, however, my meaning will be understood when I say that the recent Reform Act—which is one of the greatest revolutions, if not the very greatest, ever introduced into the British Constitution—does, in fact, bring us face to face with the need for some really potent check upon the rigid tyranny of a unitary democracy. (It was this consideration which appears to have weighed with Lord Acton.) And it seems to me that such a check can only be found by releasing certain strong, natural forces which may act as a corrective. Such a corrective will not be found in any elaborate, artificial devices, which, though they may be useful up to a point, will never really amount to much more than pea-sticks or hop-poles in a real hurricane.

There are several natural forces of this kind which I think might well be set free; and one of the most important of these certainly is the development of local powers and responsibilities within a definitely limited sphere—in other words, what we call Federal Self-Government or Devolution.

In conclusion, just a word about the powers which have been reserved to the Central Parliaments in the various Anglo-Saxon federations set up during the past 150 years.

(1) In the case of the U. S. A., the different States refused to part with sufficient powers to endow the Federal Government with adequate authority. It was only by a bold stretching of his judicial functions that Marshall, urged on by Hamilton, developed the doctrine of the "implied powers" in order to redress the balance.

(2) But even Marshall's decision was not enough for safety. The Civil War between North and South arose directly out of the deficiency of powers

15

possessed by the Federal Government.' This lesson of Civil War was fresh in the minds of men when the federal Constitution of Canada was brought into existence by the British North America Act, which is, from the federal point of view, the best constitutional arrangement of the kind yet devised. Under its enactments the supremacy of the Federal Governments is amply secured, and the State Legislatures are firmly restricted to the powers expressly delegated to them. *All unallotted powers are reserved to the Federal Government.*

(3) By the time when the federation of the Australian Commonwealth took place, the lessons of the American Civil War had been forgotten; and as a result of this unfortunate oblivion the jealousies of tne various States prevailed against the arguments of those who saw the need for Federal Parliament with ample powers. The deficiency of these powers has seriously hampered the Australian Commonwealth from the very beginning, and remains a great danger at the present day. The Australian federation is, without doubt, the weakest of all Anglo-Saxon federations.

(4) The South African Act of Union goes to the other extreme, and the reason is pretty obvious, viz., that the memory of a bitter war was fresh in the minds of those who fashioned it; they were determined, as Canada was, not to run any risks. The South African Constitution is, indeed, hardly to be called federal at all, so near does it approach the unitary principle. Personally I think this is a weakness and a danger, and may cause serious trouble in the future. The model of the British North America Act appears to be, at almost every point, greatly superior. It may also be noted that from time to time the Ulster leaders have referred with cautious approbation to the precedent of the British North America Act.

# FEDERALISM—THE IMPERIAL NECESSITY

## VIEWS OF MR. CHILDERS, MR. JOSEPH CHAMBERLAIN, AND SIR WILFRID LAURIER

Apart from the question of appeasing Irish discontent, the need for Federal Devolution, or Home Rule, has presented itself during the last half-century under two aspects. It has been viewed, on the one hand, as an essential to Imperial Unity, and on the other, as the only means for securing good government in the United Kingdom. It may not be out of place, at the present time, to consider some of the opinions which have been expressed, not in the heat of party controversy, but as the deliberate and serious convictions of statesmen whose names are held in general respect.

### OVERWORKED PARLIAMENT

The first quotation (1880) is taken from the "Life of the Right Hon. Hugh Childers" (vol. ii., p. 230) :—

"Whether time for adequately discussing at Westminster the often neglected affairs of the Empire might not be better obtained by relegating to inferior legislative bodies the purely local affairs of each of the three kingdoms, than by artificial restraints on the liberty of debate, always distasteful to Englishmen, etc. . . These impressions gained more and more power over me, and were strengthened by what I saw during annual visits to the United States and Canada. I had special facilities for watching the action of Congress and the State Legislatures in the former, and of the Dominion Parliament and Provincial Legislatures in the latter. Again and again I asked myself how is it that one race in the great Republic and in the greatest of our Colonies requires and fully occupies all this Parliamentary machinery (between 40 and 50 legislative bodies, most of them with two chambers each), while we imagine that we can adequately transact the business of England, Scotland, and Ireland, and the Imperial affairs of the whole Empire with one Parliament only? I reflected how imperfectly and hurriedly, and often badly, that business was transacted; and, referring especially to Ireland, the question constantly recurred to me whether the experiment of 1801, however needful it may have been at the time, was necessarily wise as a permanent measure; and whether, in fact, the, to my mind, cogent and, indeed, overwhelming argument of Mr. Pitt against the Parliamentary system resulting from Mr. Grattan's great change twenty years before, could not have been met, or, rather, could not now be met, in another way."

### THE RADICAL PROGRAMME

Five years later (1885) there appeared a small volume entitled "The Radical Programme." The greater part of this work consisted of articles reprinted from the *Fortnightly Review*. The preface was written by Mr. Chamberlain, who commended the work "to the careful and impartial judgment of my fellow Radicals." I am, of course, unaware to what extent Mr. Chamberlain himself was concerned in the authorship; but, judging from the clear and practical character of the arguments, I would hazard the opinion that he was not far removed from the writer's elbow. Beyond any doubt the policy set forth in the following extracts was Mr. Chamberlain's policy, and one which he consistently supported during the crisis of the Home Rule controversy, which arose a few months later. (Lord Selborne's letter in *The Times* of April 29 is sufficient confirmation of this assumption.)

### Neglect of Imperial Affairs

"Recent experience has made it perfectly clear that Parliamentary government is being exposed to a strain for which it may prove unequal. The overwhelming work thrown upon the Imperial Legislature is too much for its machinery. The enormous complexity of modern legislation, to say nothing of difficulties caused by obstruction and party politics, indefinitely postpone many measures of reform, no matter how imperatively they may be called for. The Imperial evil is not less than the domestic. What, for instance, can be more deplorable than the systematic neglect at Westminster of Colonial and Indian topics of the highest moment? It is obvious that no mere extension of local government upon the ordinary and restricted lines will relieve the Parliamentary congestion which has long since become a national calamity. Nor can it be too strongly insisted on that the supervision and control now exercised by the central authority in London involves, not only delay and difficulty in the transaction of Imperial business, but an amount of irritation and friction which is altogether superfluous." (p. 240.)

### The Conditions of Federal Devolution

"It has been well said that a problem well stated is half-solved. The problem in relation to the government of the Empire which now confronts statesmen is this—How can the work of legislation and administration in the United Kingdom be so adjusted as to secure the integrity of that kingdom, while giving to each of its component parts the best means of providing for its own public wants and developing its own resources? Such an adjustment must involve division and subdivision of labour. The Imperial Parliament cannot satisfactorily attend to its legitimate work as the great legislative body of the Empire without delegating to some other authorities the task of dealing with all matters which possess a local character." (p. 247.)

### National and Local Governments

"But when we come to consider the nature of those matters which should be included under the term local, it will be found that they are again capable of division into two classes—viz., those which affect only a small area, such as a county, and which may most properly be termed local; and those which, while affecting several *counties,* do not concern more than one of the four *countries*—England, Ireland, Scotland, and Wales—comprising the United Kingdom, and which matters might more properly be called "domestic" than "local." A National Council in Edinburgh or Dublin would be unable to undertake all the petty details of administration for every Scotch shire or every Irish county; but, on the other hand, county boards would not be bodies of sufficient weight or authority to deal with matters affecting the entire of Scotland or of Ireland, nor, from its essentially local character, could a county board deal even with any matter affecting an area wider than that over the administration of which it would preside.

18

"To make the legislative and administrative machinery of government for the United Kingdom workable it will be necessary to establish both county boards and national councils." (p. 247.)

## A Hierarchy of Governments

"By the creation of county boards and national councils we should secure in the United Kingdom a rational division of the duties and labours of government. The Imperial Parliament, the national councils, and the county boards would together form, so to speak, a *hierarchy of legislative and administrative authority,* all based upon the only true principle of government—free election by the governed. For all parts of the United Kingdom the establishment of such a system of government would be advantageous. For Ireland it would mean the beginning of a new life; it would substitute a government founded upon trust of the people in the place of one founded upon distrust and coercion." (p. 252.)

## Freedom of the Imperial Parliament

The following quotation from a speech delivered by Sir Wilfrid Laurier at Montreal in 1909 is characteristic alike of that distinguished statesman's wide Imperial and Liberal sympathies and of his delicacy in offering counsel as between one partner-State and another.

"There is one thing which always strikes me in the position to-day of the Parliament of Great Britain. It is understood that it is congested, loaded and over-loaded with petty interests and trifling questions. You may have one day in that august Assembly—the most august the world has ever seen—a discussion upon the fate of empires, or the destinies of nations, or the highest concerns of war and peace; the following day a debate upon a road ditch in Wales, a loch in the Highlands of Scotland, or a piece of bog in Ireland. The greatest possible problems that ever engaged the anxious attention of legislators and the most petty, trifling interests alternately engage the attention of the same men. There is something in this, it seems to me, not consistent with the sphere of action which ought to be reserved to an Imperial Parliament such as the British Parliament. I would not go further in this direction at present, but perhaps some time or other *some federative system* dividing legislation with regard to England, Scotland, Ireland, and Wales may be devised for the United Kingdom."

## The Danger in Normal Times

At a time when the thoughts of the whole British race are concentrated upon the issues of a great war the following sentence from "The Radical Programme" may appear somewhat startling:—

*It will be now generally admitted that the subjects of paramount attraction to the English democracy belong to the department of domestic policy, and that outside these limits it is difficult to kindle the genuine and permanent fervour of the people."* (p. 233.)

Things will doubtless be different after the war; but Mr. Chamberlain's idea (if I am entitled to call it his) was true when it was written, and unfortunately it remained only too true up to August, 1914. So long as Imperial and domestic affairs continue to be administered in the same assembly there will always be a danger, in normal times, that the former will be overshadowed by the latter.

19

# FEDERALISM—THE DOMESTIC NECESSITY

## MR. JOSEPH CHAMBERLAIN'S POLICY

I have quoted certain expressions of Mr. Childers and Sir Wilfrid Laurier, with regard to the urgency of relieving the over-burdened Parliament at Westminster. I have also quoted passages of great force, and in the same sense, from a volume entitled "The Radical Programme," which was published in 1885 under the ægis of Mr. Chamberlain. The following extracts from the same book set forth Mr. Chamberlain's views upon the need for Federal Devolution under another aspect, namely, in order that the local and domestic affairs of England, Scotland, Ireland, and Wales might be adequately considered.

### DIFFERING SYSTEMS

"The United Kingdom consists . . . of four countries, to none of which are identically the same municipal methods applicable. Let us now therefore look at the matter from what may be called the *national* point of view. The problem here is to entrust Wales, Scotland, and Ireland with the free and full administration of those of their internal affairs which do not involve any Imperial interest    There prevails, that is to say on the other side of the Tweed, a separate system of laws and administration suited to the needs and prejudices of the Scotch, and having little or nothing in common with that in force for England and Ireland. Bankruptcy, education, land laws, and many other subjects are each of them treated on an entirely different basis.

What has been said of Scotland holds equally true in the case of Wales. The peculiarities of the Welsh people, and the difference between the circumstances under which they and the English exist, give them a clear claim to exceptional domestic legislation." (p. 239.)

### COUNTY AND NATIONAL GOVERNMENT

". . . In addition to the County Boards, bodies of *national* authority and jurisdiction must be called into existence. Of these bodies, which for the sake of convenience we have called National Councils, one might sit in Edinburgh, one in Dublin, and, if the people of Wales desire it, one should be established in Wales. . . . To the *National Council* so constituted might be entrusted all the control of local administration which is necessary: the audit of accounts, the distribution of the respective shares to which the several counties might be entitled out of Imperial grants, and the contributions which such counties might be required to make towards expenditure of national importance. The work which is now performed by the Home Office, the Local Government Board, and the Education Department for Scotland and Wales, and by the Irish Local Government Board, the Irish Education Boards, the Irish Board of Works, the Fishery Board, and similar bodies in Ireland, might with advantage be transferred to a National Council responsible to the people of the country." (p. 250.)

20

"The debates in these bodies (the National Councils), dealing as they would with matters of the greatest practical interest, would occupy the attention of the Press and of the people. There would be neither room nor inclination for the minute heed which is now paid to strictly local discussions in the House of Commons. Parliament would be relieved of its too great burdens, and national life would have free scope. The political education of the people would be carried out, and the whole of its domestic business would receive the care and attention which it merits from representatives who would always be in direct communication and sympathy with the constituencies." (p. 260.)

## INJURIOUS EFFECT OF OUR PRESENT SYSTEM

"If the object of Government were to paralyze local effort, to annihilate local responsibility, and daily to give emphasis to the fact that the whole country is under the domination of an alien race, no system could be devised more likely to secure its object than that now in force in Ireland. We hold that the continuance of such a system is unjust to Ireland, useless to England, and dangerous to both. To England it is worse than useless, for while it has succeeded in irritating Ireland almost beyond endurance, it has resulted in preventing the Imperial Parliament from giving its attention to many useful reforms which England stands in need of. Englishmen will not long consent to neglect of their own affairs merely in order that they may meddle in other people's business." (p. 247.)

## EVILS OF OVER CENTRALIZATION

"A system which places the entire administration of a country in the hands of a central Government, and which divorces an entire people from sympathy with or influence upon that Government, must result in misunderstanding on one side, followed by misrepresentation and unmeasured vilification on the other. The rulers of the Castle—blindly striving to do their best for the country, which they do not, and which under the circumstances they cannot be expected to understand—complain, not unjustly, that the Irish people are unreasonable; the Irish people retort that the rulers at the Castle are tyrannical and corrupt. Under such a condition of things an intelligent and economical administration of the country is impossible. Reforms most urgently needed are not even attempted, abuses the most glaring pass unchallenged." (p. 255.)

## THE IRISH GOVERNMENT SHOULD CONTROL EXPENDITURE

"A certain amount of money is each year contributed by the Imperial Exchequer for purely Irish purposes. Surely it is for the interest of all parties in the State that the money so contributed should be employed to the best advantage. It is no gain to England to divert money from useful objects in order that it may be squandered on useless objects. Who are so likely to know the most profitable way of spending the money as the people for whom it is to be spent? Even if the Irish people should not employ the money for themselves more wisely than we employ it for them, at least they would have to blame not us but themselves for its maladministration, and for the evils arising therefrom. Irritation in Ireland against England will never die until the Irish people are fixed with responsibility; and they will never be fixed with responsibility until they have the power of electing the bodies who shall have

21

the administration of the funds raised and contributed for Irish domestic and local purposes.

"Every argument points to the necessity for not only establishing elective county boards for administering the local affairs of the county, but also for creating a *National Council* to exercise such control as must be exercised by some central body over the county boards, and to deal with domestic matters of importance too great, or affecting areas too wide, to enable them to come properly within the scope of any county board." (p. 257.)

### CAUSES OF IRRITATION REMOVED

"What is needed is that the Irish legislation should be domestic in its origin and not foreign; that it should be initiated by Irish representatives and adapted by them to the genius and requirements of the people, and that it should recognize the deep-rooted sentiment which in every nationality supports the claim for purely domestic control of purely domestic affairs.

"It is expedient, then, to recognize and satisfy, as far as may be done without danger to the integrity of the Empire, the natural desire of the Irish people to legislate for themselves on matters of purely Irish concern. . . . If they made mistakes the responsibility would not be charged to the English Government; the quarrel would be between Irishmen, and not between two nationalities. The British Parliament and the British Administration would be relieved of the thankless task of imposing benefits which are hateful to those for whose advantage they are devised—hateful more because of their origin than from any inherent defects." (p. 259.)

### CONCLUSION

The foregoing arguments appear to me to go to the very root of the matter. We need not waste time in quarreling about mere words; about whether we should call the proposed change Federalism, Devolution or Home Rule; about whether a certain constitutional instrument is to be described as a Parliament, a Legislature or a National Council. It is wiser to look at the substance of such proposals as may be presented to us, and to bother our heads as little as possible about the names which may be given to them, either by the authors themselves, or by their critics. The essential basis of what I think I am fully justified in calling Mr. Chamberlain's idea is, that Ireland, in common with England, Scotland, and Wales, should be governed for all domestic purposes—so far as is consistent with the integrity of the United Kingdom— by an Executive Ministry which would be responsible to a popularly elected Assembly.

It is said that we ought not to undertake this constitutional change at the present time during the progress of a great war. The answers to this appear to me to be two. In the first place, the evils which the change is designed to cure have been enormously aggravated—have indeed, been brought to a head —by the war. They are continuing and are growing more formidable day by day. In the second place, constitutional change cannot be attempted at a more propitious time—with a view to the thoroughness and justice of the settlement —than when the spirit of party is in abeyance, as it is just now.

So urgent is the need and so favourable the opportunity, that we should not be deterred from undertaking Federal Reform even if Ireland were unwilling at the present moment to accept it. Supposing that the South and West of Ireland should reject a federal settlement, there is no insuperable reason why the South and West should not be allowed to stand out in the meantime, and be governed more or less on the present lines, at any rate during the continuance of the war. Such a refusal would be regrettable on many grounds. Almost inevitably it must mean that Ulster would come into the Federal arrangement, like Wales, as a separate unit; and if once this arrangement were carried through it would be difficult ever to upset it.

The main consideration, however, is this—the situation of affairs in England, Scotland, and Wales being what it is, appears to render an adjustment upon Federal lines absolutely imperative, for the sake both of Imperial safety and Domestic peace. Is there any good reason why the vital needs of more than 40,000,000 of people in England, Scotland, Wales, and Ulster should be disregarded and delayed because a certain section of the Irish people persists in crying for the moon? For let it be remembered that if careful examination were possible this intransigeant section would probably be found to number something much nearer 350,000 than the 3,500,000 we hear so much about.

0 021 342 954 1

# A LIST OF IMPORTANT PUBLICATIONS
# BEARING ON THE WAR

"KNOW YOUR ALLY," with an introduction by Otto Kahn, 32 pages. Price 10c.

"TREASURY OF WAR POETRY," 289 pages. Price $1.25. (Houghton Mifflin Co.)

"THE WESTERN FRONT," drawings by Muirhead Bone—in two volumes. Price $2.50. (George H. Doran Co.)

"THE WOMAN'S PART," by L. K. Yates. Price 50c. (George H. Doran Co.)

"MY MISSION TO LONDON," by Prince Lichnowsky Price 10c. (George H. Doran Co.)

"WOMEN OF THE WAR," by Hon. Mrs. Francis MacLaren. Price $1.25. (George H. Doran Co.)

"THE LEAGUE OF NATIONS: THE OPPORTUNITY OF THE CHURCH." 28 pages. Price 10c. (George H. Doran Co.)

"THE BRITISH NAVY AT WAR," by Prof. W. Macneile Dixon. 90 pages. Price 75c. (Houghton Mifflin Co.)

"SUMMARY OF CONSTITUTIONAL REFORMS FOR INDIA." *Proposals of Secretary of State Montagu and the Viceroy, Lord Chelmsford.* 24 pages. Price 10c.

"GEMS OF GERMAN THOUGHT," by William Archer. 120 pages. Price 25c. (Doubleday Page & Co.)

"ENGLAND AND THE WAR," by Andre Chevrillon, with a preface by Rudyard Kipling. 250 pages. Price $1.60. (Doubleday Page & Co.)

"A CLEAN PEACE," by Charles A. McCurdy, M. P. 26 pages. Price 10c (George H. Doran Co.)

"ENGLISH SPEAKING PEOPLES." *Their future relations and Joint International Obligations,* by George Louis Beer. 322 pages. Price $1.50. (MacMillan Company.)

"THE VANDAL OF EUROPE,"*An exposé of the Inner Workings of Germany's Policy of World Domination and its Brutalizing Consequences,* by Wilhelm Mühlon. 335 pages. Price $1.50 net. (Putnam.)

"THE GUILT OF GERMANY," *For the War of German Aggression— Prince Karl Lichnowsky's Memorandum. Being the Story of His Ambassadorship at London from 1912 to 1914, also Foreign Secretary von Jagow's Reply.* Introduction by Viscount Bryce. By Lichnowsky. 122 pages. Price 75c. (Putnam.)

"IMPERIAL ENGLAND," by Cecil F. Lavell and Charles E. Payne. Price $2.00. (MacMillan Company.)

24

From the Press of THE CIVIL SERVICE PRINTING CO., 129 Fulton Street, New York City